The Legacy of Reverend George Allen Worley Hall And the Northern Migration of his Descendants

ISBN 9781691055609

FOREWORD

Words matter. So when CaShawn Thompson, a writer, created the concept of "Black Girl Magic" she was speaking about all Black women in America. The concept was born in 2013 as a way to "celebrate the beauty, power and resilience of Black women" as described by Julie Wilson from Huff Post, and to congratulate Black women on their accomplishments. For the Hall Gamble women, this concept brought joy, affirmation and redemption after 400 years of Black women being what Malcolm X called the most disrespected, unprotected and neglected people in America.

In this publication we celebrate the women and the men in the Hall Gamble family; but for the women it is an extra sweet time to be Black, beautiful, inside and out, loved, cherished and respected. Yes, Black Girl Magic is the spirit of Black women in America today. Let's look at why this concept means so much to all of us. As late as the early 1960s, one hundred years after emancipation, over 60% of Black women were relegated to domestic and low paying service work. That harsh reality did not stop Black women from having big dreams, achieving great things and thriving so well that today 60% of Black women are achieving in multiple arenas.

Mary Catharine Gamble Hall held a nontraditional position as a teller at the Post Office in Clow, Arkansas in the 1880's. Catharine set the tone for the Hall Gamble women to follow. Her step-daughter, Iantha Hall became an evangelist before 1920 and traveled widely to save souls. Addie Bryant, my great aunt, lived in Omaha in the 1920s, making a very good living as a caterer. She helped to pay for my grandparents and their six children to relocate to Omaha in 1923.

In Arkansas, my grandmother, Elmira taught school early as 1910 which began a long line of Hall Gamble women becoming involved in education. Janice Porter, became a librarian, Doris Foster was a Head Start teacher and her two daughters, Dr. Vanessa White is a professor at a seminary and Diane White is a speech pathologist. Dr. Janice Teyanna Walker is a former elementary school principal; Estelle Shipp and Janice Steve are retired teachers. My Aunt Susie Hall was the first Black school stenographer appointed by the Omaha School Board.

By 1940, the Hall Gamble women began stretching out into nursing studies, clerical positions and wartime time factory work. Annie Mary Scoggins was a community activist and deeply involved in the struggle for civil rights beginning In the 1950s. At the same time, other the Hall Gamble women continued expansion into nontraditional work as business owners. My mother, Iantha Hall Haynes became her husband, Millard's business partner, in their Dry Cleaning and Alterations store in Philadelphia; Ardentria Hall partnered with her husband, Charles in their Fair Deal Restaurant, in Omaha, NE; Clara Arabella Hall Norwood operated an early bed and breakfast in Indiana for family members coming North; Sylvia Hall Ransaw owned and operated a Beauty Parlor in the same area; and Georgia Hall Matlock owned a grocery store and the first gas station in Clow, Arkansas.

The next generation of business owners included Linda Green and her husband who purchased a 10 story hotel in Gary, Indiana in 1976 complete with ballroom, gymnasium and programs for inner city kids. All three of my daughters were business owners at different times in their careers. Robin L. Johnson owned a consulting business for over 20 years. Sherrie Grasty owned an insurance agency. Pamela and her husband owned an accounting and finance business. Currently, Jennifer Ransaw Smith is owner of a Personal Branding Agency called "The Personal Elevation Lab"

In the 60s and 70's Martha Hall Melton an employee of the County hospital was the evening chef, serving 1000 meals a day. Addie Hall, after studying nursing early in her career became a long time public administer in the City of Detroit, MI. Addie's niece, Jacqueline Hall worked in the nursing field her entire career. At a time when there were very few women leading Urban League chapters, Delores Hall took over as the CEO of the Sacramento, CA Urban League. By the 80s and '90s, show business was a destination for Delores Hall's two daughters, Taunya Thomas and Debra Thomas. They were models and song writers as well as performers.

Other Hall women branched out into the corporate world; Catharine Edwards is a hotel executive. Donna Monday and Pamela Johnson were bankers; Sherrie Grasty is a retired Insurance and real estate agent. Camellia Walker is a long time executive in the food industry. Karen Nared-Hood was a researcher in the pharmaceutical industry. Still, others became career government officials like Marsha Moore; or correction officers like Marsha's sister Almeta Johnson. The U.S. Marines was Karen Rose Polite-Nared's destination and she became a Staff Sargent.

Carlene Brice, Jennifer Ransaw Smith and Robin L. Johnson are all published authors. Most of all, we have returned to our roots with a new generation of Ministers of the Gospel, Dr. Vanessa White, Reverend Dr. Pam Ayo Yetunde and Minister Robin L. Johnson. We Hall Gamble Women started early following our dreams and have never relinquished our right to dream big and achieve our hearts' desires. We never accepted limitations and we wholeheartedly believe we personify Black Girl Magic.

Shirley M. Dennis
Former Director of the Women's Bureau,
U. S. Department of Labor, a Presidential Appointment

Secretary of Pennsylvania Department of Community Affairs
Commonwealth of Pennsylvania, Governor's Cabinet

Corporate Executive for PECO Energy
Philadelphia, PA , Upper Management

Retired Vice President for Institutional Advancement
Cheyney University of Pennsylvania

PREFACE

Nothing brings families together like a reunion. Once every two years we get to relax, talk and spread cheer over a three-day period. We give young kids a chance to meet and get to know their cousins, aunts, uncles and other important relatives as well as everyone else who may be new to the family – and perhaps introduce the new spouses. We are also anxious to greet older relatives who are able to attend but whose health may be in decline. There is power in a family reunion, A family reunion has the ability to reconnect families and maintain legacies for generations to come.

The Purpose

Since our first 1984 Hall/Gamble reunion in Atlanta, Georgia when we came together to celebrate a shared heritage, there have been countless milestones, fun things and accomplishments made by many of us that only a few of us know about. We realize that it may have been difficult for families to travel cross country to distance sites due to timing or financial constraints. This book is a bridge that provides a deeper understanding and insight into why the Hall northern migration occurred.

The Focus

The focus of this publication is not only to narrate the legacy of the brothers, George Allen and David Hall as they journeyed in the late 19th century from Mississippi to Arkansas but to follow the Northern and Westward migration of their descendants. With your help, what we have put together is much more than a photo album, but a historical and informative story to share and keep our family bond tight.

Sincerely,

Dr. Lee A, Ransaw, Editor
Son of Sylvia Hall Ransaw &
Grandson of Mary Catherine of George Allen Worley Hall

The Reverend George Allen Worley Hall and His Legacy

Introduction

In the first part of the 20th century, a southern flamboyant Methodist minister with steel blue eyes named Reverend George Allen Hall mesmerized his congregation, the community and the spirit of his multi-family with his engaging sermons. This book chronicles the northward and westward voyage of nine families who are descendants of Reverend George Allen Hall and his marriages to Rosie Perkins and later to Mary Catherine Gamble. These families were among many Black Americans that traveled by mule, rail, bus, and automobile in search of a better lifestyle during the period in a movement in which many called *"The Great Migration."*

During this migration, more than 6 million African Americans relocated from the rural South to the North in a movement that started in 1916 and lasted to 1970. Most of the Hall family that migrated were part of the second wave that traveled during and after World War II. They took advantage of the need in the North for industrial workers and other economic opportunities. To prepare for World War II in the early 1940s the northern factories needed laborers. African Americans who had grown weary of the segregated South saw their opportunity, and the second wave of the Great Migration began. By 1960 almost half of America's black population – which totaled at least 10 million – would live in the Midwest, West, and North. This made black Americans more urbanized, with greater access to education, entrepreneurship, and the arts.

However, the second wave of migration enflamed racial tensions in numerous northern cities, resulting in violence in the 1940s and, to a greater extent, in the late 1960s. Facing and understanding our history is very important. The Hall migration story begins with a historical review of actual events that affected the lives of our great grandparents, and thus, our lives. I have included several of my paintings which support the historical narrative. Some of these paintings have been acquired and are now part of the permanent collections at historically black colleges and universities.

CONTENTS

CHAPTER I

Narrated by Gilbert Scoggins

The Original Hall – Gamble Family History

According to our history collected by Gilbert Scoggins, we can turn back the pages of our family origin to 1834 on the Worley Plantation in Chickasaw County, Mississippi where an Irish farmer with a Scottish wife owned a number of slaves. Mr. Raven (Rayburn??) worked for him as a farm laborer and possibly an overseer. Raven cohabited with Sylvia Buckingham, a slave woman on the plantation. According to the 1900 census, Sylvia had nine children of which four were known to still be alive: George Allen Hall, David Hall, Lucy Buckingham, and Mattie Rap. The census states that Sylvia was born in Virginia. Depending on the census taker, her name is listed as Sylvia Rabun, Sylvia Rayburn or Sylvia Raven. It was known that she worked as a domestic servant after the Civil War and she lived with her daughter Lucy Buckingham and her husband Taylor in Newport, Arkansas (according to the 1900 census).

George Allen Hall was born Allen Worley and later changed his name. He was born in 1871 at the end of slavery, a free man. Two stories circulated as to how his name became George Allen Hall. One story states that one day when he went to school, a white teacher asked him what was his last name? He replied that he did not know. The teacher gave him the name of Hall. Another story states that his name was Allen Worley and that he later added Hall after his brother took the name of Hall.

Another story that was passed down was that one evening after leaving the country store, David and George were accused of stealing an item by a store owner. The next evening while they were in their barn working, the brothers looked out the window and saw a lynch-mob coming. Quickly they jumped out of the barn window and escaped into the woods. "Papa" (as George was known), put his brother David on a train heading West and they didn't see each other again until they both were grown men. Ironically, both men chose ministry as a career and both ended up in the state of Arkansas, one day "Papa" heard that over in Newport there was a good Negro man preaching the gospel named David and George went over to see him. Yes, it was his beloved brother.

THE RECONSTRUCTION PERIOD

Narrated by Lee Ransaw

George Allen Hall was born in 1871 during the Reconstruction Period just after the Civil War. Abraham Lincoln had just started planning for the reconstruction of the South during the Civil War as Union soldiers were occupying huge areas of the South. Lincoln had worked diligently to end slavery in the United States and protect escaped slaves from hate groups. He also encouraged the border states to outlaw slavery. Five years after George Allen Hall was born, Lincoln was assassinated.

In the Collection of Hampton University, Hampton, VA.

Lee Ransaw "Memories of Juneteenth" Oil 36"x 60"

In this painting, slaves have taken the fastest horse from the barn while other blacks escape by land and sea.

Congress passed the 14th Amendment in 1867 which gave liberty to recently freed slaves.

Black Codes were adopted by the Midwestern States to regulate or inhibit the migration of free African Americans to the Midwest. Cruel and severe black code laws were adopted by southern states after the Civil War to control and maintain the movements of former slaves.

The Southern "Black Codes" of 1865-66

Following the Civil War, the Ku Klux Klan emerges to suppress and victimize newly freed slaves. These goals included the political defeat of the Republican Party and the absolute maintenance of white supremacy,

THE HALLS & GAMBLES – A METHODIST CONNECTION

It is well known that the Halls and Gambles have had a strong connection with the Methodist church. Colored people, as they were called in the early years of the Methodist church, included in its membership all races, creeds, and colors. They can be traced as far back as 1768 in Arkansas where 30 colored people and a few Indians faithfully worshiped.

Much of the land along the Arkansas, Mississippi, White, Ouachita, St. Francis, Red, Cache, and Fourche Rivers, made rich farmland and many slaves were brought in to help raise the increasingly profitable cotton crops. The first Methodist preaching in Arkansas was said to have been by an ordained local deacon, William Stevenson, who helped to establish small congregations among early settlers. Some of his travelings carried him 125 miles South into **Ozan** and **Clow**, Arkansas in Hempstead County. His preaching was the first in Arkansas under the guidance of a presiding elder or bishop.

Richard Norris Brooke 1847-1920 "The country preacher makes a home visit"

THE SPIRITUAL IN SONG AND STORY

In 1836, Arkansas was admitted to the Union. At that time, there was no separate provision for holding services for colored people who frequently were permitted to attend white people's services, occupying seats assigned to them in the rear, or in overhanging galleries of the church, which were out of sight of the main congregation. On other occasions, sometimes on Sunday, the coloreds could use the master's place of worship for one service, if the master felt so inclined. Religion had presented the slaves with the idea that they would receive their reward after they died. This appealed to their minds, but they were not necessarily convinced that the way to heaven was through obedience to their owner, and sometimes they questioned the notion of the heaven it promised with reward only in the afterlife. This caution was sometimes expressed through spirituals. The term spiritual is used to categorize the complete body of Afro-American religious songs created during the slave era. For a long time, it was theorized that spirituals were conceived solely from a narrow religious perspective that was aligned with the black man's understanding of Christianity. However, there were other events that affected the creation of his music such as physical abuse, inadequate living conditions, and the desire to be free. Some spirituals sometimes suggested that justice would be meted out to the oppressor and that there was a formula for actually achieving freedom.

In the spiritual "*I Want To Be Ready*" the surface material expresses belief in and hope for eternal life.
I *want to be ready.*
I want to be ready.
I want to be ready to walk in
Jerusalem just like John.

Clow, Arkansas in 1870 was an all Negro-town. It was described as having a population of 2,559 (Mine Creek-Clow). This growth was due mainly to the migration of Blacks coming from other southern states and the Oklahoma territory. Some came searching for family members who had been sold during slavery while others looked for jobs and a better living condition. The rail line that served the town was the Missouri Pacific Railroad. The Gambles were among the early families that migrated to Clow. Not much is known about their history except that Oscar and his sister Nannie, both born in South Carolina were taken from their parents at a very young age and sold into slavery. They never remembered their parents. The name Gamble was given to them by whites. After the slaves were freed, they made their way to Arkansas. During this same period, Lincoln was trying desperately to get the states back together. This was also during the Reconstruction Period between 1860 – 1880 when Negroes were celebrating the passage of the Fourteenth Amendment granting them citizenship and equality. Many whites sold or simply left their land and moved away. Many Blacks were given key jobs, some without training. Oscar Gamble became the 1st Black Postmaster in Clow. He also became a powerful man and landowner.

Vernice Gamble, also the son of Oscar Gamble Jr., became the 1st Black Loan Officer for the FHA in Arkansas. In Clow, he met Clara Arbella and to this union bore the following children.

1. **Mary Catherine Gamble**
2. **Robert Gamble**
3. **Rayfield Gamble**
4. **Mathew Gamble**
5. **James Arthur Gamble**
6. **Drayton Gamble**
7. **Queen Ann Baker Gamble**
8. **Lee Emma Gamble Carr**
9. **Willie Bell Gamble**
10. **Elizabeth "Sis" Gamble Scoggins**
11. **Ellis Gamble**
12. **Parthena Gamble**
13. **William Gamble**
14. **Oscar Gamble Jr.**

One day as Oscar Gamble was returning home from shopping, he remembered that he forgot to get a ham for dinner. As he attempted to get off the train, he fell, severely injuring his leg. There was no doctor there to amputate, gangrene set in and he soon died.

Sojourner Truth

Sojourner Truth, born Isabella (Belle) Baumfree (circa 1797-November 26, 1883) was an African American evangelist, abolitionist, and author was active during George "Papa Hall's" lifetime. She lived a miserable life as a slave, serving several masters throughout New York before escaping with her infant daughter to freedom in 1826. The year 1834 was the turning point for Truth. She became a Methodist, and on June 1, she changed her name to Sojourner Truth. Around 1815, Truth met and fell in love with a slave named Robert from a neighboring farm. Robert's owner (Charles Catton, Jr.) forbade their relationship. He did not want the people he enslaved to have children with people he was not enslaving because he would not own the children. One day Robert slipped over to see Truth, and Catton and his son found Robert and savagely beat him. Truth never saw Robert again. Truth eventually married an elder slave named Thomas with whom she bore five children.

Lee A. Ransaw *"Sojourner Truth presents Abraham Lincoln with a Bible"* Oil on canvas 24"x30"

My painting above shows the day (October 29, 1864) that Sojourner presented President Lincoln with a Bible from the Colored people of Baltimore. *"He took my little Book with the same hand that he signed the death-wish to slavery."*

Lincoln wrote:
"For Aunty Sojourner Truth"
October 29, 1864

Abraham Lincoln

CHAPTER II

Narrated by Shirley M. Dennis, daughter of Iantha Hall Haynes

Rev. George Allen Hall and Rosa Perkins Marry

George David Hall was the first born to the union of Rosa Perkins and George Allen Hall who married on January 19, 1885, in Panola, Mississippi. The couple was living in Mariana, Arkansas when George David arrived on September 13, 1888. Three other children were born to this union, Samuel, Rosemon, and Iantha (for whom my mother, Iantha Hall Hayes was named).

Rev. George Allen Hall and Mary Catherine Gamble Marry

On September 18, 1899, Mary Catherine Gamble and Rev. George Allen Hall were married. Mary Catherine helped Rev. Hall to raise his four children for nearly 5 years before she had her first child, Freddie. Little did anyone guess that George Allen Hall, Rosa Perkins Hall and second wife Mary Catherine Gamble would produce a total of 16 children and numerous grand and great-grandchildren.

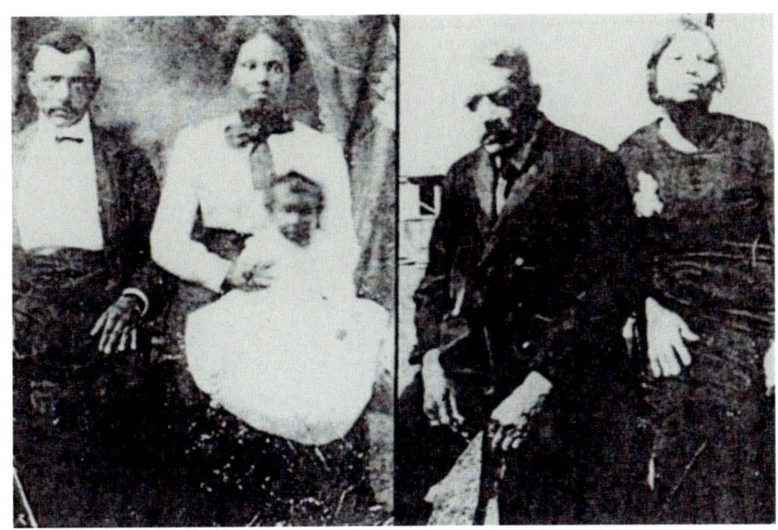

Early 1900s **Early 1930s**

The Patriarch – *Reverend George Allen Hall*

Rev. George Allen Hall

The Wedding Portrait 1910

George Jr. and Elmira Bryant Hall

George David Hall attended seminary for two years before marrying Elmira Bryant. He was preparing to follow in the footsteps of his father and uncle, Rev. David Hall. George and Elmira were married on August 1, 1910. George owned a store and they settled in the area of Horatio, Arkansas and began their family. Percy, Iantha, Susie, David, Charles, and Martha were born before trouble with whites signaled the need to leave the South. Percy beat up a white boy in a dispute and George was a little bit too prosperous, owning his own home and business which made the family a target for jealous whites in the community. This was a common problem for blacks during those years and many moved North to protect their families.

***Purchased by Coppin State University*, Baltimore, MD.**

Lee A. Ransaw "The Scottsboro Boys" Oil on canvas 30"x40"

There was also trouble for some Blacks while moving North. By the 1930s, when the nation was stuck in the Great Depression, racial injustice raged throughout the deep South. Many unemployed Americans would try and hitch rides aboard freight trains to move around the country searching for work. On March 25, 1931, after a fight broke out on a Southern Railroad freight train in Jackson County, Alabama, Police arrested nine black youths, ranging in age from 13 to 19, on a minor charge. But when deputies questioned two white women, they accused the boys of raping them while onboard the train. They were transferred to the local county seat, Scottsboro, to await trial. In 1932, The Alabama Supreme Court upheld the convictions of seven of the defendants, most were sentenced to death. Years of court battles followed in an effort to free them. Some were freed.

Omaha, NE was chosen as the destination for George and his family because Elmira's older sister, Addie and her husband were living there. Addie sent bus tickets for Elmira and the 6 children ages 11,9,7,5,3, and 6 mos. George arrived several months later after settling his business ties. The family struggled in Omaha to get back on their feet financially. In Arkansas, Elmira was able to teach, and George was a businessman. Neither of these options was open to them. They were able to find work, but it was menial and did not pay enough to assure prosperity to a family of eight even though this was the roaring twenties and jobs were plentiful.

In spite of low salaries, the family had many happy times. They were blessed with good voices and sing-alongs were common in their household. They joined Clair Methodist Church; George grew lush vegetables so there was always plenty of food. The family also grew in size adding two girls, Addie and Delores before Elmira caught pneumonia and died in 1935. At the time of her death, the three youngest children were 11,9, and 6 years old.

Iantha and Millard Haynes Meet and Marry

This narrative is about the branch of George David Hall's first daughter, Iantha Gertrude Polly Hall Haynes and Millard Haynes. They met as teenagers, when Millard migrated from Pensacola, FL to Omaha, NE where Iantha had lived since her family migrated from Arkansas in 1923. Millard came to Omaha to learn a trade in which he later became an expert. His work as a tailor was so good that he made his own clothes. His expert tailoring extends to making clothing for my mother, friends, and customers.

Iantha and Millard married in the middle of the depression, July 1, 1935. Two daughters were born to the union before World War II and Millard was drafted. He was sent overseas to North Africa for three years. During Millard's time in the military, Iantha continued as a surrogate mother to her three younger sisters following the death of her mother. When Millard received his Honorable Discharge, he wanted to move to New York City. My mother was reluctant to leave her family that depended upon her, but they assured her they would be fine. So, the family of four, Millard, Iantha, Barbara and Shirley moved to New York City in 1945.

LIFE IN NEW YORK CITY

Our first home in overcrowded New York City was sharing an apartment with family friends in Harlem until our new housing was built in the Bronx. When the Haynes family moved to the Bronx, there were few Black families in their new community. In fact, Barbara and Shirley were two of only four Black children in the elementary school. Prior to moving to New York, the sisters attended an all-Black school and playmates were mostly cousins and children of close family friends. Making friends in the new community was much more of a challenge. Shirley often speaks of "lessons learned " like to thrive as an "outsider." Shirley says that lesson has served her well in life and career.

Reverend Adam Clayton Powell, Jr.

Three years later the family moved back to Harlem. This time to a new high-rise public housing on 132nd Street and Park Ave. They attended Abyssinian Baptist Church whose Pastor was none other than Reverend Adam Clayton Powell Jr., the renowned Congressman from Harlem.

Iantha and Millard along with the girls were active socially and culturally. New York offered many wonderful activities, such as theatre, parades, festivals, amusement parks, cruising on the Hudson River, live shows at the Apollo, dancing at the Savoy, programs at the nearby City College and much more.

Barbara and Shirley both attended progressive public schools. Barbara learned clothing design and alterations from school and her father. Upon returning from the Army, Millard attended NYU, studying clothing design and pattern making. He then secured work in the garment industry on Seventh Avenue, altering and making clothing for the wealthy. Shirley went in a different direction. She showed oratorical skills early and coupled with her interest in Civil Rights, her course was set.

Moving to Philadelphia

In 1952, Millard moved his family to Philadelphia because he had an opportunity to purchase a dry cleaning and alterations business in North Philadelphia. Barbara and Shirley both were in high school at that point. They worked in the business after school. Barbara did alterations. Shirley waited on customers. When Barbara graduated from Dobbins High School, she obtained a position in one of the high fashion stores doing alterations before marrying David Nesmith and becoming a housewife with four children, Gale, Lisa, Gary, and Wayne.

Barbara and David are both deceased. All of their children remained in Philadelphia. The two boys have a total of seven children, Gale and her husband, and Kelvin have two girls, the names of the children are according to birth order; Zakia, Jasmine, Sheena, Ieasha, Mercedes, David, Khyeerah, Roxanne and Terrell. Lisa and Carnell do not have any children.

When Shirley graduated, she received a one-year scholarship to what is now Cheyney University of Pennsylvania. She then married college classmate, Marshall L. Johnson. Three children were born to this union of five years. They were Pamela, Robin, and Sherrie. After the divorce, Shirley went into real estate sales and took her first steps into public life. The firm that she worked for was called Tucker and Tucker and was owned by a young active black couple. They along with Shirley's parents became role models for her future life and career. Delores Tucker (of Tucker and Tucker) later became the first black woman to be Secretary of State in Pennsylvania.

Shirley Haynes Johnson becomes Shirley M. Dennis

William D. C. Dennis and Shirley Johnson met at Abington Presbyterian Church in 1965. It was a fair housing meeting and a mutual friend orchestrated a way for Bill and Shirley to meet, although neither was aware of the plan. Even though Bill and Shirley knew a number of the same people, were active in the NAACP and both sold real estate, they did not know each other. Bill drove Shirley home and a new life began for the two of them, although it took three years for them to get on the same page, marry and begin the joint work of a "Power Couple."

During 1965, Shirley was the key witness for the City Human Relations Commission on housing discrimination resulting in a new Fair Housing Law passed in 1967 by the City of Philadelphia. She testified for the State Housing Law passed in 19967 by the City of Philadelphia. She testified for the State Human Relations Commission in 1966 and the State passed a companion Fair Housing Act in 1968, the year Bill and Shirley married. With God at the center of their relationship, they embarked on a 50 year plus journey of supporting and making many changes in their community at the local, state and national levels. Bill holds an associate degree from Temple University in drafting and is a former builder. In the 1970s he became an elected official in Abington Township. He also opened a Real Estate Agency on property that the two owned. Shirley became the President of the local NAACP and CEO of a non- profit housing advocacy agency.

By the 1980s Bill was President of the Board of Commissioners of Abington Township (in cities this position is called a Mayor). They hosted Dr. Martin Luther King, Jr. Holiday programs at the Township government building and Shirley headed the Pennsylvania State MLK, Jr. Holiday Commission in her role as Secretary of the Department of Community Affairs for the State of Pennsylvania (a part of Governor Dick Thornburgh's Cabinet.)

Shirley Dennis Swearing-in Ceremony at Department of Labor

Robin, Martha Melton, Shirley and Bill, Sherrie and Lee Ransaw

Shirley holds an associate degree in Business from Temple University; a BA from Cabrini and an MBA from West Chester University; a Fellowship at Harvard University's JFK School of Government and two Honorary Doctorates; She was also honored with a Presidential appointment to become Director of the Woman's Bureau for the U.S. Department of Labor. Later she was an executive for PECO Energy and Vice President for Institutional Advancement for Cheyney University.

The Daughters, Pamela, Robin, and Sherrie Come into Their Own

The Dennis' daughters, Pamela, Robin, and Sherrie are college graduates. All three received their BA's from what is now Clark-Atlanta University. Robin received a fellowship to study for her master's degree in Paris and London. When she finished her program, Pamela, Sherrie, and Shirley traveled to London and subsequently, the four of them traveled to Paris, Brussels, and Amsterdam. Over the next 40 years, the four traveled together and apart to nearly 50 countries and Shirley to all 50 states of the United States.

Robin went back to Paris for her 2nd MBA degree in International Affairs. She became conversant in French, making travel to France most enjoyable for mother and daughters. Robin owned a consulting business for over 20 years. She is a Minister of the Gospel, a Spiritual Life Coach and an author of two books, *Awakening of a Chocolate* Mystic and *ETA to Oneness.*

Pamela finished Clark with a BA in Finance. She married Phillip Peoples and they have a son Jonathan. She and Phillip owned a Financial Advisory Firm for several years. After their divorce, they remained good friends and successfully co-parented their son. Pamela later worked in Banking, her first love, insurance and a number of other private sector businesses. She also worked for The Grasty Allstate Insurance Agency, owned by her sister Sherrie. After retiring, she became a foster grandparent and currently is the guardian of Jonathan's son, Symir Taylor.

Sherrie received her BA in Finance and returned home to Abington Township and began a very productive career at Allstate Insurance Company as an adjuster. She married Lorenzo Grasty. They have two sons. Marcus and Myles. Both sons attended college but are still seeking long term careers. In the meantime, they are gainfully employed, and each has one child, Marcus, a son named Zacharay; Myles, a daughter, Aysa.

Sherrie became a consultant to other adjusters while at Allstate and was there for over 30 years before embarking on a business ownership at the same location where Bill operated his real estate business for 30 years. Sherrie and Pamela put in many long hours before Sherrie decided that she wanted to go in a different direction. She closed the insurance agency down right at the time she became a grandmother. She enjoys the grandchildren beyond her wildest dreams. Grands are truly the reward for surviving your own children.

THE DENNIS GALLERY & ARCHIVES

Robin & Shirley in China

Robin at Taj Mahal, India

Sherrie & Robin

Doris Foster in Rome

The Honorable Shirley Chisholm, Coretta Scott King, and The Honorable Shirley Dennis share a special moment

Sherrie & Lonnie on 25th wedding anniversary in Maui, Hawaii

The Dennis Family

A Philadelphia gathering

Sylvia, Bill, and Shirley Dennis

Addie Hall, Iantha G. Hall, Janice Hall Porter, and Shirley's father - Millard Haynes

Billy & Martha Melton

Shirley Broadcasting over World Net

CHAPTER III

The Foster Family

Narrated by Dr. Vanessa White

Coretha Hall- Mother of Doris Jean Foster

FROM CLOW TO CHICAGO

Coretha Hall, the ninth child from the marriage union of Mary Catherine Gamble and George Hall, was born in November 1915 in Clow, Arkansas. She met Virgil Redd while both were students at Philander Smith College (A Historically Black College in Little Rock, AR.) in the early 1930s. Virgil Redd was the son of Amelia and Lloyd Redd of Popular Grove, Arkansas. After a courtship, they were married in 1933 and moved to Virgil's home in Popular Grove. A year later, Coretha gave birth to her first child, Doris Jean on January 7, 1934. Unfortunately, soon after the birth of Doris Jean, Coretha became ill with a stomach ailment that doctors were not able to diagnose. She later died in October from complications of this illness. Her daughter Doris was 9 months at the time. (Story goes that she was also pregnant at the time with her second child).

Coretha was buried in Clow, Arkansas. Doris Jean was then raised by her father, Virgil and paternal grandparents, Amelia and Lloyd Redd. Doris recounted that she was later told by her father that Rev. Cortelyou Clifton Hall (Coretha's brother), wanted to adopt Doris and stated to Virgil that he could give her a good education. Uncle CC (as he was affectionately called) later became an esteemed member of the United Methodist Church in the Little Rock Jurisdiction. Doris states, "My father and his parents would not hear of that because they felt that they could do the same."

Doris Jean Foster

Doris shared that she met her maternal grandmother, Mary Catherine Hall when she was 14 years old. At that time, she also met her mother's sister, Sedalia. She shared that she "loved her grandmother on that very first visit." A few years later she met her mother's siblings – her Aunts-Arbella, Sylvia and Uncle CC at her father's house when they came to visit in Popular Grove, Arkansas. She became closer to 'Aunt Sylvia who wrote her letters and sent her school clothes during her high school years. She came to know her "Aunt Sedelia" when she started classes at Philander Smith College in 1952. At that time, "Uncle CC" was on the Board at Philander Smith College and he would come to visit her and take her to visit her Aunt Sedelia.

Mary Catherine Gamble Hall and Sylvia Hall

While attending college, Doris met her future husband, Robert Lee White from Chicago, when he came to Popular Grove with Doris' uncle, Floyd Pippins. Her father had remarried to Mary Pippins and Floyd was her brother. Over the next two years, through letters and visits, they fell in love and were then married. Robert (known as Bob) then brought Doris to Chicago, IL. In December 1954. At that time Arbella (her mother's sister) lived in the neighboring city of Gary, Indiana and was a tremendous support to Doris, while Robert traveled on the railroad as a cook.

Doris has been a loving wife (Robert Lee White (d. 1966) and Herbert R. Foster (d. 1980) and mother giving birth to three children. Coretha "Vanessa" White, who was named after her grandmother (b. 1956) and Diane Sylvia White (b. March 12, 1959) and Herbert Randolph "Randy" Foster (b. June 18, 1967) (m. Erica Sewell). She is grandmother to Anaya & Tosha and great-grandmother to Breanna, Cedric, and Darius.

The Fosters – "Randy," Doris, Vanessa, and Diane

The Foster Family Achievements

- **Doris** went on to complete her education at Prairie State College where she received an Associate degree in Early Childhood Education and taught in the Head Start Program in Harvey, Il. She has been a strong advocate for education. Her children also have gone on to further their studies.

- **Vanessa** has pursued theological education and ministry with a Master's in Theology and received a Doctorate in Ministry from Catholic Theological Union in Chicago.

- **Diane** has pursued theater and speech pathology with a Bachelor's in Theater (Illinois State University) and Master's in Communication Disorders (Governor's State University).

- **Randy** has pursued supervisory construction work in the utility field with a Diploma in Electrical Maintenance from Coyne College. His grandchildren continue the legacy of furthering their education and pursuing their passions in their work and studies.

Vanessa, Randy, and Diane

THE FOSTER PHOTO GALLERY AND ARCHIVES

Doris Jean Foster and Family

Doris Jean in Rome

Uncle CC & Aunt B.

Shirley & Vanessa

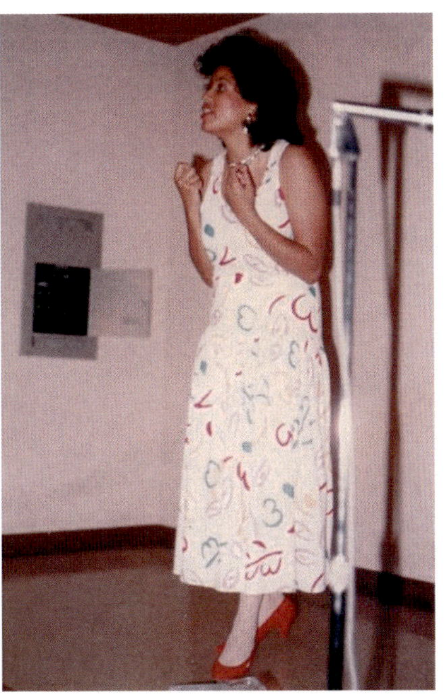

Diane in performance

Rev. CC Hall and family gather at George's funeral

Clara Arbella, Rev. CC & Aunt B, "Buddy," Maxine, Xynipher & Freddie Hall and Aunt Odessa Hall and George Hall II, Kneeling.

Diane, Jennifer and Vanessa at Lee's reunion gathering in Atlanta

Virgil Redd, Coretha's husband and Mary Catherine Gamble 1934

Mary Catherine Gamble

Rev. CC Hall's church in Fort Smith, Ark.

CHAPTER IV

Narrated by Dr. Lee A. Ransaw

The son of Sylvia Hall Martin and Grandson
of
Rev. George Allen Hall & Mary Catherine Gamble

Sylvia Hall Martin

Clow was founded by freed slaves and was once a community of 2,500 black landowners. Bowen Seminary for Black students was founded in Clow in 1890. Negroes owned and operated all enterprises. They were trained businessmen. Mr. Oscar and Mr. Eli Gamble operated a grocery store, another grocery and general merchandise store, and post office were owned by Mr. Price Jones. Mr. John J. Johnson operated the drug store and Dr. Gozier was the dentist. The flamboyant Reverend George Allen Hall was one of the pastors that served the community. Vernice Gamble, the son of Oscar Gamble Jr., became the 1st Black Loan Officer for the FHA in Arkansas, a position that he held until his untimely death. The eldest daughter of Oscar Gamble was the beautiful Mary Catherine Gamble who worked as a teller in the Post Office. After he lost his first wife Rosie, Reverend George Allen Hall set his eyes on Mary Catherine Gambel whom he courted and married in 1899. To this union, they bore twelve kids.

Rev. George Allen Hall and Mary Catherine Gambles' Children

1. Freddie	5. Cardie	9. Coretha
2. Sedelia	6. Georgia	10. Arbella
3. Cortelyou	7, Oscar	11. Sylvia
4. Cortelyou Clifton	8. Clarence	12. Xynipher

Two boys, the first Cortelyou and Oscar and one girl Cardie died at a very young age.

There were many children growing up in Clow, as well as in Hempstead County. Large families were important because it allowed them to harvest their own crops. However, these small towns only provided a secondary school for Negroes and the Methodist families that desired better education for their children. The A.M.Es' decided after slavery that they wanted to have their own schools. After much discussion, they put their talk and desires into action. They raised sufficient funds to erect a school that offered high school and normal courses. They were assisted financially by the Clow District of the Methodist Episcopal Church. This new school was named Bowen Seminary in honor of Dr. J.W.E. Bowen, Sr. father of the late Bishop J. W. E. Bowen, Jr. Bowen had a home for girls, operated by Mrs. Catherine Gamble.

Bowen Seminary was financed by student fees and district funds from the M.E. Church. Students came from three neighborhood grade schools and surrounding towns. There they were prepared to teach and to preach. Bowen Seminary also served as a feeder school for Philander Smith College in Little Rock, and Wiley College, in Marshall, Texas. It closed in the early thirties due to lack of funding and nearby high schools.

Sylvia Ann Hall, my mother, was the youngest girl of the offspring of George and Mary Catherine Gamble Hall. She was born in Clow, Arkansas in 1918 and she decided at an early age she was going to make something positive happen in her life.

S

Sylvia at seventeen

This photo was taken when she was 17 years old as she was about to graduate from high school. While in high school my mother was very active and played on the basketball team. After her graduation from high school, she planned to enroll in college, but being from such a large family with six brothers andfive sisters. she didn't have the funds to pay for her classes, so she pawned her high school class ring to pay for several courses at Philander Smith College.

SYLVIA ANN HALL WEDS LEE ANDREW LESTER

While taking courses at Philander Smith College, Sylvia was courted by a gentleman by the name Lee Andrew Lester. His brother was the Rev. W.D. (Woodie Daniel) Lester who was an author and a well-respected Methodist preacher. Rev. Lester was also the father of the social activist and Newbery Medal winner in literature, **Julius Lester** whose books included **To Be A Slave** and "**Look Out Whitey! Black Power's Gon' Get Your Momma."** Julius Lester was my 1st cousin on my fathers' side. He recently passed. (1939-2018).

Lee Andrew Lester was a teacher, a coach, and a tailor. Later in his life, he became an ordained minister who would later help build churches in Arkansas and Louisiana. He would tutor Sylvia in mathematics as she prepared for her classes at Philander Smith College. When they married, Sylvia moved from Clow to North Little Rock, Arkansas, and to this union had their only child together, Lee Andrew Lester, Jr. He made all of my clothes. However, Lee Lester Sr. and my mother divorced several years later. She began making plans to raise me in the North.

THE NORTHERN MIGRATION TO "THE PROMISED LAND"

Jacob Lawrence '*Heading North* 'Panel #42 Gauche on Board

Chicago, a city Blacks called both ***The Promised Land*** and ***Heaven on Earth***, was desperate for black labor and guaranteed steady work to thousands who flooded there from the American South. Jobs were plentiful and social institutions such as schools and churches flourished. In panel #42 of the Migration Series by the renowned artist Jacob Lawrence, he portrays a black family, after picking up their last pay from the southern landowner, purchasing a one-way train ticket heading for the industrial North in search for better jobs and a new life. Often families would dress up in their Sunday best for the voyage and pack baskets with enough food for the entire trip.

During the war years, Clarence, Arbella, Freddie and Xynipher Hall, three of Sylvia's siblings had already moved North to Gary, Indiana. Several Gambles including Leslie, Rayfied, and Reginald had also migrated to Gary. It's not clear who arrived first. There were plenty of job opportunities in the steel mills of East Chicago and Gary, Indiana. Because of the war, there were also many factory and industry jobs available for women. Xynipher Hall had been honorably discharged from the military and married Marjorie LaBroi. Uncle Clarence married Hazel Broadnaux and uncle Freddie married Odessa Wiley. Everyone encouraged my mother to join them.

Sylvia Hall Begins a New Life

Recently divorced and with a small child, my mother had to put together a plan. She went to an older brother, Rev. C.C. Hall told him of her plans to join her sister and brothers in Gary, Indiana. He questioned her ability to raise a four-year-old child in Gary without having a job. He first offered to adopt me, promising to give me a good education and send me to Philander Smith College. Mother refused this offer. Afterward, he promised to keep me until she found employment. Mother accepted this offer and took the Union Pacific train and headed for Chicago, Illinois and then the bus to Gary, Indiana. She moved in with her sister Arbella and Leroy Bailey.

Clara Arbella Hall at 18

HALLS & GAMBLES IN GARY

Arbella *had moved to Gary, Indiana and she and Leroy Bailey adopted an infant girl from her sister Georgia Hall Matlock, named her Virginia. They later adopted Shelia and Michael.*

Freddie and Odessa Hall's *children were Maxine and Freddie Jr. (Buddy).*

Rayfield and Amy Gamble's *children were Charles (Conrad) and Hershel Lee.*

Xynipher and Marjorie LaBroi's *children were Rosemond & Janet Hall.*

Clarence Hall *did not have any children.*

THE HALL BROTHERS

Xynipher Hall

Clarence Hall

Freddie Hall

Rev. Cortelyou C. Hall

In Gary, Sylvia found work and over the next two years, saved her money, enrolling and graduating from a beauty school. With the aid of Madame C.J. Walker's hair products, well-trained beauticians made a comfortable salary.

Sylvia Hall, seated at the left on the front row graduates from beauty school in Gary, Indiana around 1943.

Sylvia returned to Arkansas, thanked her brother C.C. and his wife aunt B. for keeping me and subsequently brought me back to Gary, Indiana. Uncle CC later helped me with my college tuition at Indiana University.

I remember that the really early years of my life in Gary were filled with fun. We had plenty of food and family gatherings. Virginia was like a sister to me. Mother enrolled me in an elementary school not far away from my 1st grade. Serious crime was very low, and the neighborhood was safe. Perhaps it was because World War II had ended, and everyone was happy. Parents were able to do things then that are unthinkable today. For example, we lived close to downtown and a movie theater. Mother would take me to the theater to watch the adventures of Mighty Mouse and other cartoons. She would walk me down to the first or second row, give me a box of Cracker-Jax with the prize inside, and instruct me to remain there until she returned for me. She would then go shopping and faithfully return to pick me up an hour and a half later and we would stroll home. When mother had to go to work, I had to walk alone across a large sandlot to get to school. She would pin my gloves and house key to my jacket so I wouldn't lose it, there were no school buses then and many other kids walked to the all-Black grade school alone. We felt entirely safe. Uncle Xynipher Hall, who was a barber by trade, was my favorite uncle during this period. He would come over to our apartment and we would get on the floor and he would draw these wonderful flowers and birds. That experience stuck with me over the years.

"*Momma Hall*" Visits us in Gary, Indiana

World War II had ended and my Grandmother, Mary Catherine Hall paid a visit to us in Gary. Mother and uncle Clarence Hall decided to dress up for this family photo. I guess I must have been impressed by the war and uniforms, so I'm photographed wearing this navy uniform. This photo was shot on Valentine's Day in 1945. Pictured are aunt Hazel and uncle Clarence with my mother on the back row. On the front row, I'm standing between "*Momma Hall*" and another aunt.

Aunt Hazel, Uncle Clarence my mother on back. Myself, Grandma Hall and another aunt on the front row

Sylvia Hall Lester Weds George Ransaw

George Ransaw, a young insurance salesman met and began courting my mother, and they both decided to marry. He wanted to leave Gary and move to Indianapolis, Indiana where his sister and her husband lived. They had recently moved into a large home in an integrated neighborhood on the north side of Indianapolis. This is where George proposed that our family life together would continue. However, to be assured that this arrangement would work with me, once again mother decided to go to Indianapolis alone with George. Since I had started school, she arranged with aunt Arbella and Uncle LeRoy to keep me in Gary until the school semester was over. That summer mother brought me to Indianapolis.

Life in Indianapolis

Mother had no trouble gaining employment as a beautician on famous Northwestern Avenue. On "The Avenue" which stretched for more than 30 blocks was the C.J. Walker building and a theater where the famous Ink Spots first began their career, night clubs, Crispus Attucks, the only black High School in the city, plenty of jazz and numerous thriving black businesses. Before I entered the 4th grade, mother legally had my last name changed from Lester to Ransaw. Mother had a vision. After divorcing Lee Lester, she recognized that she had to leave the South for a better life for both of us and find a better educational environment for me. A couple of years after I moved to Indianapolis, we moved into another house two blocks away. Janice Matlock came up from Clow and moved in with us until she was able to find employment and get her own place. A few years Later Virginia Bailey moved to Indianapolis from Gary.

Lee Andrew Ransaw

Since I was living in this newly integrated section on the north side of Indianapolis (which was only about a 10 square block area), I was among the first black children allowed to attend the recently integrated, predominantly all-white Shortridge High School. During the 1940s and 1950s Shortridge High was ranked among the top ten high schools in America, it patterned itself after Duke University with same school colors and mascot. It had its own radio station and daily newspaper. However, within those walls, there was deep segregation, no black girls could become cheerleaders, and no more than three blacks could be on the varsity basketball, tennis or baseball team. Since the football team wore helmets blacks could play any position except quarterback." The classes were tough and demanding and it wasn't until my junior year before I attained the confidence that I could cut it. I was sitting in an English class which was 95% white when the teacher gave us an assignment to go home and learn *The Preamble to the Constitution.*

Two days later she asked who could recite the *Preamble*. Several tried, but no one could successfully do it, so I raised my hand. She called on me and I got up and, obviously to her and my classmate's amazement, I flawlessly recited it. The following week she assigned the class another oral report to memorize the first six verses of *The Constitution*. Again, I was the only one who successfully recited it on the first day. For me, receiving that educational experience from Shortridge High School paid off. However, I owe much of this to my education success to the wonderful teachers from the all-black George Washington Carver Elementary School (PS 87) that I attended who prepared all of its' students well.

Thanksgiving Family Gathering in Gary, Indiana

Arbella, Shelia, Leroy, Sylvia, Janice, Virginia and Jerry

EDUCATIONAL ACCOMPLISHMENTS

As I mentioned earlier, uncle Xynipher was influential in my interest in pursuing the visual arts as a career. I received both a bachelor's and master's degree in fine arts from Indiana University in Bloomington, Indiana. The summer that I finished my master's degree I married Patricia South of Indianapolis and to this union, Jennifer and Lee Andrew, Jr. (Randy) were born. After teaching for three years in Louisville, Kentucky I accepted a teaching job at, believe it or not, at Shortridge Junior High School in Indianapolis. After teaching there for three years I was transferred to Arsenal Technical High School, become the first black art teacher in the city of Indianapolis teaching art at the high school level other than the all-black Crispus Attucks High School.

In 1970, I received a Ford Foundation Fellowship to pursue a Doctorate degree in art and Arts Administration at Illinois State University. Pat, baby Jennifer and I packed up and moved to Normal, Illinois. Patricia received a scholarship from the Communication Department to work on her master's degree. We both graduated together. Randy was born in Atlanta, Georgia. It wasn't long before Patricia and I divorced, and she moved back to Indianapolis. A number of years later in Atlanta, Georgia I married Cheryl Johnson, who now serves as Director of Diversity and Chief Human Resource Officer at Georgia State University.

Teaching in Higher Education

- The **University of Wisconsin** in Madison. was my first teaching assignment in higher education. There were more than 30,000 students there, Patricia gained employment as a news broadcaster at a local TV station while we were there.
- **Morris Brown College,** Atlanta, Georgia – Department Chairman and Dean of Arts & Letters. (Professor Emeritus)
- **Emory University, Atlanta,** Instructor -Art History Department
- **Spelman College, Atlanta.** - Adjunct Professor - Education Department

Professional Accomplishments

- **UNCF Distinguished Scholar** to study abroad for one year
- **Rockefeller Foundation Fellowship** to the Metropolitan Museum of Art,
- **Ford Foundation Fellowship**
- **History Makers of America** – Chicago, IL, HQTRS,
- **100 Black Men of America** Member
- **Founder of the National Alliance of Artists from HBCUs**
- **Organized 1st Hall Gamble Family Reunion** in Atlanta, GA in 1984
- **Hampton University: Guest Editor** of the International Review of African American Art Hampton, VA.
- **Board of Directors**, The APEX Museum in Atlanta, GA.
- **Board of Directors,** The National Conference of Artists
- **Author of two textbooks**: including *Below the Surface: Ethnic Echoes in Contemporary Art & The Art of Black Music*

LEE'S PHOTO GALLERY & ARCHIVES

Great Pyramid Of Giza

research trip to Paris

In Tangier with Muhammad

Lee & Jennifer in Haiti 1976

The Great Stonehenge

Cheryl & Lee at Harlem Renaissance Gala in Atlanta

In Amsterdam with fellow artists

Cheryl & lee on cruise

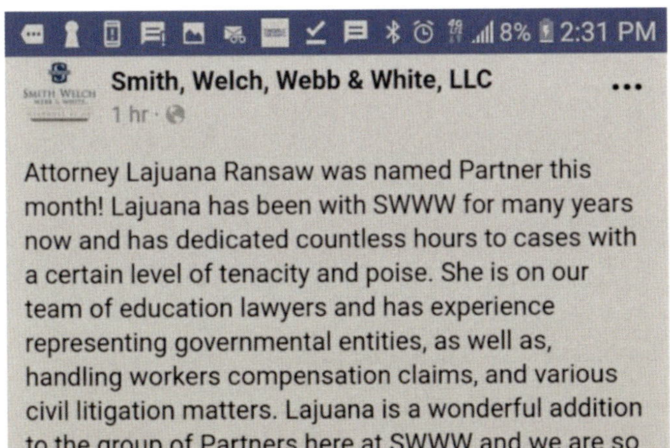

8% 2:31 PM

Smith, Welch, Webb & White, LLC

1 hr ·

Attorney Lajuana Ransaw was named Partner this month! Lajuana has been with SWWW for many years now and has dedicated countless hours to cases with a certain level of tenacity and poise. She is on our team of education lawyers and has experience representing governmental entities, as well as, handling workers compensation claims, and various civil litigation matters. Lajuana is a wonderful addition to the group of Partners here at SWWW and we are so proud of her!

Lee" Randy" Ransaw. Jr. and his wife are having successful careers. Attorney Lajuana has been promoted to a major law firm and Randy is a Mid-Manager with Delta Airlines in Atlanta, Georgia.

Dean of Arts Letters at Morris Brown College

Cheryl & Lee at New Year's Eve Bash

Lee in Rio de Janeiro, Brazil at National Art Conference

Mexican Pyramid -The Teotihuacan

Teotihuacan wasn't just a religious temple; it was a city. No one knows who built it. It had at its peak, 20.000 people living there.

Jennifer featured on a billboard after delivering the keynote Address at College in South Carolina, 2018

The Halls, Sylvia, Arbella, & Charles reunite with family in Omaha

Lee and Randy with artists and educators in Oslo, Norway

Cheryl Ransaw and sisters Jaye Sandford and Charis Johnson

Lee and son Randy in Copenhagen. Randy is a Mid-Manager with Delta Airlines

Jennifer Ransaw Smith with family: Husband Fred, Kendall, Payton and Bailey Smith

- Jennifer's career in advertising has taken her to Los Angeles, Maryland, Washington, D.C. and New York City. She has written radio, television, and print for some of the nation's most recognizable brands including Burger King, AT&T, Kraft, Clairol and Texaco.
- She went on to head the PR Department for Newsweek Productions and eventually launched a career in Personal Branding.
- Fred has been appointed a Vice-President at Master Card in the DC area

CHAPTER V

Narrated by Linda Green

The Migration of Addie Hall

Addie Hall Gilmore

Addie migrated to Detroit, Michigan from Omaha in 1951 with only a high school diploma and two children, Ricky and Linda. She worked hard. and purchased her first home in the late fifties. Later, in the sixties, Addie enrolled in Michigan State University and received a degree in social work and went on to get her master's degree. She worked long hours on improving the quality of life for low-income families.

She was Director of Head Start Programs in Detroit, Mich. for many years. In addition, she worked in neighborhood services, child development, and community services. She also worked on the research study of "The Impact of Head Start" on parents and children.

Mother shared her love, wisdom, and finances with family and friends. All of her life she tried to be of service to others.

************** **I miss her greatly** **************

Linda, Addie, and Ricky

LINDA'S GALLERY AND ARCHIVES

Berkeley California reunion

Doris Jean, Ricky, Almeta, Camilla, and Janet

Susie Kemp, Martha Melton, Addie Hall, Delores Hall 1947 Omaha, Neb.

MY BROTHER RODERICK

In 1968 my brother Roderick (we all called him Ricky) went into the military. In 1972, however, he came out on a medical discharge and for the rest of his life, he lived with one illness after another. Ricky never married and had no children. For awhile, he lived in Gary, Indiana with me.

Ricky

REFLECTIONS OF OMAHA

There was no place like "The Fair Deal" restaurant located on 24th Street in Omaha, Neb. Our Uncle Charles Hall, the owner, always provided great food and music. The Fair Deal was known as the "Black City Hall." It was the essence of an individual in this city owning and successfully operating his own business.

New Year's Eve gathering at Fair Deal Café

Top Left Janie, Melba, Martha, Susie, Herman
Front- Delores and Addie

The love you felt was overwhelming and the pride, "Oh My!!!!" On Sundays, Claire United Methodist Church was where the Hall family worshiped for over 100 years and its reputation was well known throughout the United States.

Aunt Susie, Martin Luther King, Jr., and Delores – a historic photo-op

Percy Bryant Hall

Percy's family which included Janice and her brothers

The Three Addie's –Addie Terrell, Aunt Addie, Cousin Addie

FROM DETROIT TO GARY, INDIANA (LINDA'S JOURNEY)

Linda Green

Detroit was a hard city to grow-up in without family there. Ricky and I looked forward to going to Omaha every summer. Upon arrival, we were greeted like royalty by all the elders. Uncle Charles, Aunt Dennie, Aunt Martha, Uncle Billie, and Aunt Janie plus all of our cousins. We would stay with dear Aunt Susie and Uncle Herman who cared for us like a mother and father would and with much love.

PROFESSIONAL ACCOMPLISHMENTS

- I moved to Gary Indiana, from Detroit, Michigan in 1970 with two children, Donald and Donyale. In 1972 I married Raymond Green who was a businessman. During the summer of 1976, Raymond and I purchased a ten-story hotel in downtown Gary on 5th Ave called the Kay Cee. The building had a ballroom, bowling lanes, and inside swimming pool, a gymnasium and a basketball court. We sponsored low-income children ages 7-12. There were also organized buddy basketball, pee wee football, and baseball teams.

- In 1975-77 we were instrumental in getting the first Black State Senator elected in Northwest Indiana. In 1978 we worked closely with Senator Rudy Clay in sponsoring and getting a bill to the Senate floor for a Martin Luther King, Jr. holiday. Although at that time it did not pass the Senate, Raymond and I continued working on social issues for many years.

- In 1982 I managed my own business for the next 10 years, and in 2000 I took a position with the Geminus Corporation. I have been retired since 2015.

Young Linda Green

USA TODAY Featured Linda

...not the same feeling when you see armed police ...ing down every boulevard or when you're searched every time you enter a store."
— *E.D. Barnes, Santa Barbara, Calif., tourist in Paris*

"This gray September, beneath the rain, beneath the bombs, fear has arrived in Paris."
— *French journalist Dominique Jamet*

ONE LINE ON THE NEWS

■ In addition to a $78,000 salary, Clemson coach Danny Ford gets "fringe" benefits worth hundreds of thousands of dollars and a 137-acre farm in 1995.
How else can you keep him down on the farm?

...the terrorists and jeopardize the lives of innocent people.

Such stories generally fall into one of two categories:

■ Reports of ongoing or imminent operations designed to strike against terrorists and/or rescue hostages.

■ Reports of plans for broader-based operations to fight terrorism.

In the first category, we find all of the reports about the movements — real or imagined — of U.S. military or paramilitary units to the scene of a terrorist incident. Many of the networks announced early in their anxiety, heighten the risk to the hostages, and make any rescue effort more difficult.

In like manner, imagine that a U.S. network had broadcast — a few hours before the bombs fell — that our warplanes were heading toward Libya. This would have given the Libyans time to prepare and endangered U.S. pilots.

In the second category are the various stories about alleged U.S. "covert" operations aimed against regimes that sponsor international terrorism — like Gadhafi's. Such stories make it far less likely that make their tasks ... more dangerous and difficult.

The news media should certainly learn as much as they can and prepare to inform the public; but they should wait until the event is over before "going public" with such stories.

The public's right to know does not require that it know everything at once. Indeed, both the public interest and the national interest are better served by a calmer approach: The stories are likely to be more accurate, and the people fighting terrorism will have had a better chance to succeed.

...ganized terror's ... ence on govern... ally friendly t... highlighted.

Instead of t... which would ... warplanes ove... battlegrounds i... thousands fron... fighting in two ... of the French, ... forced to tak... around. The ... ment turned it ... as not to offen... guinary and f... which, in this ...

VOICES FROM ACROSS THE USA/Should pre-emptive strikes and military retaliation be use...

***DONALD JANKURA**, 56*
Hotel executive
Parker, Colo.

I would hope that there would be another way to combat terrorism without using military force. All countries have to increase their security measures in monitoring the people entering and leaving their countries. Until we find out who the terrorist groups are, we cannot do too much to fight terrorism.

***LINDA GREEN**, 36*
Business owner
Gary, Ind.

Pre-emptive strikes and military force should be used to stop terrorism. They both show that the USA will not put up with terrorism. Terrorists have gotten out of hand. If they're not stopped soon, things will start happening in the USA. Negotiation doesn't do any good. Retaliation is the only way to deal with terrorists.

***BARRY HAMM**, 22*
Food catering captain
Peoria, Ariz.

Pre-emptive strikes are extreme acts to take to combat terrorism because they could possibly start another war. Perhaps our military men who are stationed in foreign countries should watch for possible terrorist acts to prevent them from happening. I would not want the U.S. military to go out and fire first.

***MARJORIE PADGETT**, 52*
Pharmacy technician
San Diego, Calif.

I worried at first when the USA retaliated against Libya, but later I thought retaliation was the right thing to do. Our bombing of Libya set terrorism back a bit. It made the terrorists stop and think. Retaliation will not stop terrorism, but it will make terrorists realize that if they act against us again, the USA will strike back.

***WILLIAM UTNIK**, 65*
General manager
Atlanta, Ga.

The USA should take strong, immediate action against terrorism, but not military action. Someone at our military bases overseas should be in charge of immediately evaluating a terrorist act to determine how we should handle it. No action should be taken until after an in-depth evaluation. There has been enough killing already.

BETSY BRO...
Communicat...
New York, N...

If we knew ... who the ter... where they ... yes, we sho... only would ... people direc... we would b... sage to othe... thinking of a... we absolutel... if we're unce...

USA Today New Paper

The Blessings of The Lord has helped me in all things.
Praise God

Linda Green

The Fair Deal Cafe

Aunt Dennie, Uncle Charles and Donna Monday, his daughter

Billy & Martha Melton, Sylvia Hall Martin & Terri Lynn who tragically departed much too early

Dee Thomas with Stevie Wonder

Omaha archives

Janet Hall & Swainge T. Gibson

Sylvia & Arbella going fishing

Dee, Arbella, Shelia, and Taunya

CHAPTER VI

Narrator - Carleen Brice

Granddaughter of Martha Melton

Carleen Brice and husband Dirk Dickson

Carleen is the daughter of Leroy Brice and the granddaughter of Martha Melton. She holds a degree in journalism from the University of Kansas, and since 2013 she has worked in the marketing department at the Denver Art Museum. She lives in Denver with her husband Dirk Dickson, a bass player.

PROFESSIONAL ACCOMPLISHMENTS

- **Carleen Brice's** debut novel, Orange Mint and Honey, was an Essence "Recommended Read," a Target "Bookmarked Breakout Book" and a Denver Post bestseller. Alicia Keys said of Orange Mint and Honey, "This is the reason I love to read. This book has so much character and wealth of soul."

- In February 2010, Orange Mint and Honey premiered on the Lifetime Movie Network as "Sins of the Mother," starring Jill Scott and Nicole Beharie. It was the second-highest rated original movie in LMN's history.

- Her second novel, Children of the Waters was a book about race, love, and family. It also hit the Denver Post bestseller's list. Jacquelyn Mitchard, author of the Deep End of the Ocean said "I was exhausted and singing the blues the hour I began Carleen's new novel Children of the Waters. Five hours later, I'd finished this fresh, free-rein novel about mothers' secrets and children's sorrows and was shouting "Hurray!" Booklist Online called it "a compelling read, difficult to put down." AOL Black Voices said, "Brice sparkles with a tale of love and family."

- **Carleen** is also the author of two nonfiction books, Lead Me Home: An African American's Guide Through the Grief Journey and Walk Tall: Affirmations for People of Color, which sold 100,000 copies. She edited and contributed to Age, Ain't Nothing but a Number. Black Women Explore Midlife. She has written for *The Washington Post, The Denver Post, The Chicago Tribune, Poets and Writers and Mademoiselle.*

- She is the recipient of the 2009 First Novelist Award from the Black Caucus of the American Library Association and the 2008 Break-Out Author of the African American Literary Awards Show.

CHAPTER VII

The Porter Family's Migration

Narrated by Janice and Donna Porter

Donna and Janice Porter

Percy Bryant Vandyke Hall was born August 31, 1912, in New Port, Arkansas to George David Hall and Elmira Bryant-Hall. His father, George, was 23 and his mother Elmira was 21. He was the eldest of his siblings, Iantha, Susie, Charles, David L., Martha, Addie, and Delores. Percy was about 17 years when the family moved to Omaha, Nebraska. By the time Percy was 22, he had met and married a beautiful young woman named Melba Lee Robbins. They were married in Council Bluffs, Iowa on March 14, 1935. They would go on to become parents to Janice, Percy Jr., Charles, George, Guy, and Gary.

Percy had a love of music and he joined a quartet called the Southern Breezes, singing as a tenor vocalist. The group would perform in small joints in Omaha. They had signed a contract offered by an Omaha radio station. However, due to WWII, the quartet was forced to end after only a year or two, because two of the members were drafted.

Janice, Percy Bryant Hall, Percy Jr., Melba Lee, and Guy

In order to support his growing family, Percy had worked odd jobs, including bartending, before landing a position as a waiter on the Union Pacific Railroad. Although it required a considerable amount of travel, it also provided Melba an opportunity to be a full-time mom.

Percy B. Hall worked as a waiter on Union Pacific Railroad

A BRIEF HISTORY OF THE FAIR DEAL CAFE

The Fair Deal Restaurant in Omaha was purchased early in 1953 by Clifford Robbins, Melba's father. Melba Hall and brother-in-law Charles would assist in cooking at the Fair Deal. While Janice was a senior at Omaha Tech high school, sadly Clifford Robbins had a stroke in May of 1953. However, on his deathbed, he offered and sold the Fair Deal to Melba for $1. Together, Charles and Melba would run the restaurant until the end of October 1953.

After Percy's lifelong friend Booker Gordon moved to California, he convinced Percy to move his family there, So the Hall family moved via Pacific Union Railroad for free. They were given all their meals, (3 daily) and bedding for free as well. It was a wonderful experience for the whole family. After the family arrived in Los Angeles, Percy decided to end his 17-year employment with the railroad due to route conflicts. Percy convinced Melba to turn the Fair Deal over to his brother Charles because the family had no plans to return to Omaha.

Percy worked various jobs until he landed a job at Wiltshire Country Club in the clubhouse as well as working as a bartender. **Fun fact**: Johnny Carson, the television personality, ran into Percy at an event that Percy was working. He approached Percy, recognizing him from his bartending days in Omaha. They talked for quite a while, and whenever Johnny Carson saw him at an event bartending, Johnny would stop and chat with him. Percy worked at the country club for nearly 8 years until his death in October 1966. Percy and Melba were married for 31 years. Melba passed away on April 12, 2000, in Gardena, Los Angeles, California.

PERSONAL ACHIEVEMENTS

- ❖ **Bryan Porter** – Judge in Chicago's Municipal Court & Attorney.
- ❖ **Janice Porter –** Head Librarian at Bauder College in Atlanta for 18 years. Holds a Master's degree from Chicago State University.
- ❖ **Donna Porter** - Graduated from Georgia State in Criminal Justice & was a Court Bailiff.
- ❖ **Arleta Porter-** Comptroller at the University of Chicago and a graduate of Spelman College with a degree in Accounting.
- ❖ **Alexis Porter-** Student at Spelman College majoring in Accounting.

THE PORTER PHOTO GALLERY AND ARCHIVES

Janice, Hazel and Sylvia at Arbella's house party in Gary, Ind.

Janice, Arleta and Lee

Alexis Porter

Arleta, Bryan & Alexis

Donald Porter

Alexis Porter at Spelman College

Arbella, Donna and Dominique Porter

The Porters with two Past Presidents of Spelman College

Percy Bryant Hall and wife

Alexis, Arleta & Judge Bryan Porter

CHAPTER VIII

THE LIFE AND LEGACY OF DELORES ELMIRA HALL

Narrated by Terrence "Max" St. Thomas

Delores Elmira Hall and Addie Hall

Delores Elmira Hall, born in Omaha 1930, was truly an exceptionally bright star. As a result of several marriages, not only was she the mother of four loving and bright offspring, but she was a trailblazer that opened political doors, opportunities within the radio and television industry, and for Black women in general. While in Omaha, Delores married Lonnie Benjamin Thomas. He helped to raise Lonnie Jr., Deborah Thomas, Terrence "Max" St. Thomas and Delores Taunya Bryant. Lonnie Sr. and Delores divorced in 1960 while all were still young. Taunya was an offspring from an earlier marriage to Robert Bryant.

Taunya, Lonnie Thomas Sr., Deborah and Terry "Max" St. Thomas

Delores worked for many years at the Omaha public libraries setting up a new system but was noticeably replaced by a "white manager" at each library that she helped reorganize. Each time she was relocated. She became ambitious and in 1960 left Omaha for Denver, Colorado.

Lonnie Thomas Sr.

Lonnie Sr. worked at the Omaha Douglas county Courthouse as a county assessor for 26 years before his retirement. I believe that the only thing that Lonnie loved more than his family was golf. In my opinion he was the Tiger Woods of that time because he won sooo many golf tournaments (black only). Golf in the 1940s was still a white man's game, but Lonnie worked his way thru the ranks starting as a caddy at the local golf Clubhouse. He took the abuse but learned the game and earned numerous victories on the Black circuit. Eventually winning the newly formed "Central States Golf Tournaments that included entrants from 5 Mid-West States and solidified his place in history as 'one of the best' of his era.

After their divorce, Delores moved to Denver, Colorado to pursue her ambitions. Though he and Delores divorced about 1960, they loved us so much that they allowed us, the children, to always decide with whom we wanted to live, with their mother or with their father. The two girls moved to Denver with their mother while the boys stayed with their dad.

In Denver, Delores obtained her bachelor's degree at the University of Denver and soon remarried and became Delores Curvin. Affectionately known as "Dee," she began wearing a number of hats; a school teacher (educated and educator) in the Denver Public School system, a "Probation Officer" for troubled teens, and hosting many community projects including fashion shows. She knew prestigious people in the city and soon purchased a large beautiful house on Monaco Parkway. Delores was also an excellent artist, selling a number of her paintings in galleries to patrons and friends.

Delores Hall was also an artist and sold her paintings under the name of Delores Curvin. Here, she is admiring a work by David Colbat in an exhibit in which she also participated.

Through the 60s she entered the political arena including democratic party rallies., equal rights activities and some interactions and meetings with M.L. King Jr. and Sr. (See Delores with Martin Luther King, Jr, on Page 60). At the height of her political career there she was very articulate in putting together and presenting to Denver City officials a massive housing project for the underprivileged that she named "Model Cities" which was initially rejected. (Note: a few years later and without her getting ANY recognition, a 'similar' project was fully funded & developed and renamed "Montebello.") In 1969, after running unsuccessfully for the House of Representatives, she married for a third time to an Air Force Academy graduate and I relocated with them to his base in Sacramento, CA.

It was Sacramento where she began to fully flourish. As Executive Director of the Sacramento Urban League. There she created a refreshing environment of community self-help programs. But she eventually experienced pure degradation via political hardball. Through the 70s, she worked hard presenting the Urban League's motto to promote equality, destroy discrimination and build up the minority class. The more she achieved these goals, the more she was attacked from within by her own organization, The National Urban League under their then President, Vernon Jordan. I remember the many nights she came home in tears, seriously questioning "why, why, why are they doing this to me." Referring to what she called a "Kangaroo Court" of the national charter attacking her tactics of pursuing and obtaining equipment & property which was mostly 'donated' to her chapter to assist in her goals to achieve equality.

Vernon Jordan and his 'goon squad' relentlessly accused mom of 'stealing' equipment. I lived with her in those years and personally know there was no cache of typewriters or office equipment. Obviously, there was an incredible amount of jealousy that a small black woman with an above average drive for excellence from Omaha, Nebraska could amass such notoriety and achieve so much in a highly influential environment as the California State Capital. Jordan felt threatened by her popularity and achievement and did what he could to crush her integrity. (Not a well-known fact, but I was there to experience it with her.)

Unfortunately, in 1979 Delores succumbed to a massive heart attack while in California. Although she was only 49 years of age, her funeral was solidly attended by not only family & friends, but also by a large arena of national politicians who acknowledged her significant work.

Dee Thomas

Dee Thomas is a multi-faceted songwriter, and voice artist who is comfortable in the world of music whatever the genre, Country, R&B, Rock & Roll, Hip Hop and more. A Midwesterner, this writer grew up in different regions of the country exposed to lots of music, dancing in night clubs as a child, performing on the same shows with greats before she was legal. She opened for Al Green with her own band as a kid, a whole coliseum cheering her on. Hanging with the promoters, asked by Bobby Blue Bland and his band," You wanna go to the party?" she replied, "I have to go to school in the morning." Even hanging around Ester Phillips and Sarah Vaughn, she's always been down to earth with a pulse on the people. She later became lead singer with George Duke.

Dee has written and sung for film and television soundtracks. Parent Trap III, being one her most fun credits. Growing up on stage, she's performed Billy Holiday, Dinah Washington, *Lutibelle* in "*Purlie*!" and others. Having done commercials for Heineken and more. She also became a featured singer with Lionel Richie performing the hit Endless Love and recording on many of his hit songs.

Dee Thomas holds a BA degree in English and Sociology. She has extensive study in Journalism and songwriting, with much experience working with children, and encourages their creativity and personal growth.

THE THOMAS PHOTO GALLERY AND ARCHIVES

by Dee & Terry Thomas

Charles "Butch" Brice & Sharon

David Lee Hall, Jr.

Dee sang at the 90th birthday of the great tapper Fayard Nicholas, of the Nicholas Brothers and the honoring of the movie Stormy Weather

Debbie in concert

Duet with Lionel Richie (Jet Mag.)

Duet with George Duke

Taunya as a centerfold in Jet Magazine

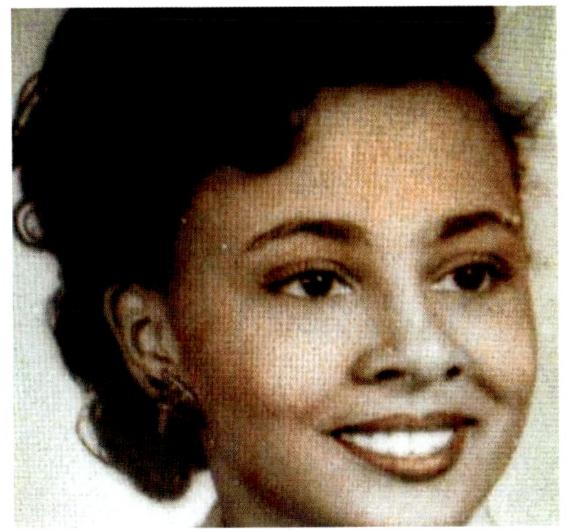

Martha Melton

The Halls with George Hall in Omaha

Lonnie Thomas Sr. with golf trophies

Billy Melton – The Music Man

Dee Thomas

TAUNYA (aka Empyrst) flashes her sparkling chameleon green eyes

Taunya, like my brother Lonnie Jr. graduated from the school of hard knocks. She also left the fold at an early age to pursue a life of lavish luxury, which with her bubbly personality she easily achieved. After her time in high school in Denver, she moved to the San Francisco Bay area (Sausalito) and then to Los Angeles and to another level of prominence. She appeared in the centerfold of ***Jet Magazine***. She not only had a radio program but also became a Vice President of Marketing in the highly successful "Pre-Paid Legal" business.

Terry, Dee and Lonnie Jr.

Dee, Lee, and Taunya at a Los Angles National Arts Gala

TERRY "MAX" ST. THOMAS

To this writing (New Year's Eve 2018-19) I am sitting in a Truck Stop awaiting the New Year in my 18-wheeler. I have been trucking for about 6 years. After about 45 years of working in transportation. I'm finally making the most money I've ever made working. I am self-employed, solo driver and twice divorced without children. I've had about 50+ jobs through my life (always liked having money, just didn't like the job to get it! Lol.) To name a few achievements.

- Air Force (crew chief on world's largest aircraft C-5A).
- Omaha Police Officer
- Professional photographer
- Currently professional driver in the oilfields of West Texas

Terry "Max" St. Thomas

MORE PHOTOS FROM THE THOMAS ARCHIVES

Dee and singer Oleta Adams

FROM DEEP IN THE ARCHIVES

Elmira Bryant on her wedding day

CHAPTER IX

The Westward Migration of the Scoggins

Narrated by The Scoggins Family

Annie Mary Scoggins (affectionately called Ann) was born March 5, 1928, in Clow, Arkansas. Clow was established in the 1860s as a small African American agricultural community in Hempstead County. Ann's parents instilled in her a strong belief in God and the teaching of Jesus Christ.

Annie Mary Scoggins

Ann was the eldest of ten siblings and two extended family members: Bobbi Matlock-Campbell, Janice Matlock-Steve, Lizzie Matlock-Walker, Virginia Matlock-Pinner, Feazel Matlock Jr., Stella Matlock-Ship, Bertram Matlock, Freddie Matlock, Wilbur Brown, and Georgia M. King.

During her formative years, Ann lived off and on between Clow and Hot Springs, Arkansas with her aunt Arbella. Ann attended Philander Smith College, a private historically African American, four-year undergraduate liberal arts institution located in Little Rock, Arkansas. She excelled in college, majoring in English. Philander Smith was established by the Freemen's Aid Society of the Methodist Church in the late 1800s to make education available to freed slaves and was one of the founding members of the United Negro College Fund. Note Alumna: Joycelyn Elders, former Surgeon General of the United States.

In the mid-1940s through the 1960s the entire country, especially the southern states were going through a new paradigm shift. The Civil Rights Movement was born and began to challenge the racial disparities in the treatment of people of color. This was especially true on issues that involved racial discrimination in housing and employment, as well as the inequality in education.

HEADING WEST

In 1948, ***Ann*** married Alphas Scoggins of Clow, Arkansas. Four years later, with two children, Alphas Jr., and Gilbert, the Scoggins joined the African migration from the poor economic conditions and Jim Crow laws of the South to various cities in the North and West. In 1954 Ann and her husband relocated to Berkeley, California where they eventually purchased a three-bedroom home under the GI Bill. Alphas Sr. began employment with the Naval Supply Center in Oakland, California, and Ann briefly operated an in-home hair styling business. Between 1949 and 1961, her life was enriched with eight children: Alfas Jr., Gilbert, Georgenia, Margie, Harold, Angela, Windy, and Gary.

The Scoggins Family

Although California presented better economic opportunities, the Scoggins family was not prepared for the marginal living conditions they found. Here, people of color continued to experience unequal treatment, institutional racism and filtered civil rights challenges from the White establishment. Ann could not stand by silently. Thus, she began her journey as a grassroots civil rights organizer and ultimately became a passionate champion for equal rights. This became a life-altering decision and to this end, Ann decided to devote her time to Public Service.

Ann was well known throughout the West Berkeley community for her amazing ways of extending kindness to everyone. She had a special way of reaching out to the women in her neighborhood, who were also struggling and seeking a means to improve their families living conditions. Ann was very proud of making her home a safe place where women could gather and openly talk and pull together their resources to help one another in need. This effort continued to grow into other areas as the challenges of the day grew. She set out to take a leadership role towards positive change efforts for the betterment of underrepresented low-income communities.

Alfas Scoggins Jr, and Gloria Scoggins in Vegas

Accomplishments

- In 1960 Ann and Alphas Sr. founded the West Berkeley Neighborhood Council. The mission of this non-profit was to empower the community to become politically charged to address the issues that were impacting their daily lives. Ann worked diligently on the front-line advancing integration in the Berkeley Unified School District.

- In 1963, inspired by Dr. Martin Luther King Jr., Ann put her rigorous community activism toward organizing the first Poor People's March in the City of Berkeley. Ann's commitment and due diligence towards such causes encouraged many others to also take a stand.

- In 1968 Ann met and consulted with Robert F. Kennedy and the Ambassador to the United Nations during their bay area campaign. Kennedy assured Ann that, if elected President of the United States, he would help.

- In 1970 Ann met with the Warden of San Quentin Prison in San Rafael, California to discuss multiple issues, including prison reform and solutions to social problems.

- In 1980 Ann founded the Caring and Sharing Program, designed to provide services for the "Neediest of the Needy." As Founder and President, Ann's mission was to provide referrals to needed resources, including clothing, food, shelter, and prayer. Ann enjoyed making sure that the homeless in her community were never excluded. They affectionately called her "Mama Scoggins." Every Thanksgiving and Christmas she hosted a banquet and festivities for homeless and low-income families.

- In 1984 Ann was invited to be the keynote speaker at the Hall/Gamble Family Reunion in Atlanta, Georgia.

- In 1987 Ann became a board member on the Religion of the World Conference and participated in its conference held in Marin County where she met and conferred with Yogesh Gandhi, son of Mohandas K. Gandhi.

Additional Accomplishments

- Director of the Intercultural Training & Development Center, Berkeley, CA
- Board member on the War on Poverty Program, Berkeley, CA.
- Originated the basic concept entitled "Giving All Children a Head Start in Life" which was adopted by the Berkeley Unified School Board in 1963.
- Vice President of the Columbus School Parent Teacher Association (1964)
- Teacher's Aid, Operation Head Start Program.

- Sunday School Teacher, Westminster Presbyterian Church, Berkeley, CA.
- Student Exchange Program adopted in 1964 by the Berkeley Unified School District Board.
- Board member, Berkeley Unified School District (1965)
- Founding member and teacher, Basic Adult Education Program, Berkeley, CA.
- Director, Intercultural Training & Development Center, Berkeley, CA.
- Member Easter Star Fraternal Organization,
-

Several years before her passing in 2006, Ann was faced with several health problems that limited her mobility. This lack of mobility did not hinder her ability to get things done. As she once said, "The great contribution that I have ever made has been to volunteer my services towards one humanity."

THE SCOGGINS GALLERY AND ARCHIVES

Gilbert Scoggins, Randy & Lee Ransaw with Troy Walker

Roman & Family

Robin & Angela

The Scoggins Family

Angela Scoggins

Wendy Scoggins

Fallen Scoggins & family

The Scoggins Family

Vegas Reunion

Gary and Jackie Scoggins

CHAPTER X

The Migration of the Matlocks
Narrated by Estella Matlock Shipp

This is a little about
"The Life of the Feazel and Georgia Mary Hall Matlock's Family"

Feazel Matlock, Sr

Georgia Matlock

Both F**eazel** and **Georgia** were born in the vicinity of Ozan and Clow, Arkansas. I'm not sure of the exact locations. To this union were born 10 children, six girls, and four boys. Annie Mary Scoggins, Bobbie Mae Campbell, and Bertram James Matlock are deceased.

Feazel, Georgia and five of their children left Clow. AR. For Memphis, TX in 1950. Feazel joined his sister, Essie Matlock Starr as she and her husband Jimmie had some experience and knowledge of farm work in that part of Texas. Shortly after leaving Memphis and moving to Hale Center, TX, my dad became a sharecropper. He had a position in which he had the authority to hire or fire people that he had been entrusted with. He helped hundreds of people to get on their feet. Going there to work helped us get ahead financially. Life became much better in every way. Money was saved from our work, which made returning to Clow more prosperous and less stressful for our parents. The 5 children that went to Texas with them in 1950 had become adults and gone their separate ways. We learned from our parents that hard work pays off. We also learned to never be ashamed of what you do as long as do it honestly. Church was very important in helping to shape our values and keeping us on the straight and narrow path.

Annie Mary Matlock Scoggins went to Philander Smith College for several years. After she married Alphas Scoggins they relocated to Berkeley, California. They were the proud parents of 8 children. Bobbie M. Matlock Campbell married Alfred C. Campbell and moved from Clow to Luxora, Arkansas. They are the proud parents of 5 children. J**anice Matlock Steve** was married to Joe Steve. Janice attended Philander Smith College 4 years and received her BS Degree. She worked for a short time in the Indianapolis School District. She left Little Rock, AR for Indianapolis, Indiana in 1954 after graduating from Philander. Her first marriage was to Alonzo Coleman. She was the proud parents of two boys.

Lizzie Jean Matlock Walker was born September 14, 1933, and after graduating from high school, she married her childhood sweetheart Troy Walker and both moved to Berkeley and Oakland, CA. for a better lifestyle. They are the proud parents of 5 children. She worked at Manzanita Elementary School for 25 years before her retirement. Troy became employed at the Naval Supply Center where he worked for 35 years, When my five children (Reginald, Gerald, Camellia, Donald, and Daryl) became older, I started working for a Convalescent Home, and then later started a career with the Oakland Public Schools where I worked as a cook for over 20 years.

Feazel Matlock Jr. left Clow in 1949 for Hale Center TX, and in 1960 moved to Gary, Indiana. He retired from the Steel Mill after 34 years of service. He and his wife Rosa Briggs were the proud parents of 4 children. Ronald Matlock later moved to Gary, IN, while Bertram J. Matlock, remained in Clow.

Ron Matlock, Troy, and Lizzie Matlock Walker

Virginia Pinner R. Pinner was raised by Aunt Arbella, so she lived most of her younger years in Gary, IN. She married Curtis Pinner and they were the proud parents of 2 children.

Virginia Matlock Pinner

Troy & Lizzie Walker

Aunt Sylvia, Camilla, Freddie and Feazel Jr. in Hot Springs for fresh spring water

Ronald, Bertram and Feazel Matlock, Jr.

Estella Matlock married John Mathew Shipp, Jr. in 1962 in Little Rock, AR. I married Mathew after graduating from Philander Smith College, receiving a B.A. Degree in Elementary Education and later a master's degree from Texas Southern University,

Clarence Hall

Clarence Hall, son of Mary Catherine Gamble migrated to Gary, Indiana as a young man. He admired the lifestyle of the upward mobile young black men in and around Chicago and quickly adopted their flair for fashion and hairstyle.

Feazel Matlock Jr., in GQ

Estella Matlock Shipp

Front row: Janice, Virginia, and Bobbie- Back Row Estella, Burtam, Freddie & Feazel Jr.

Ron Matlock and friend on a cruise

Janice Matlock Steve with painting

Estella, Ron & a friend

CC Hall as builder

Not only was Uncle CC Hall a District Superintendent and a minister who pastored churches in Hot Springs, Hope, and Fort Smith, Arkansas, but he also served on the Board of Directors at Philander Smith College in Little Rock, Ark. Rev. Hall was also an astute business man and a builder. He constructed and owned 15 homes that surrounded his house at 250 Walnut Street in Hot Springs, Arkansas.

Troy, Lizzie, and Camellia

Ruby Briggs Matlock, Barbara Gamble and Shelia Bailey in lower right corner

Ron, Vanessa, Camellia, Lee, Doris Jean, and Cheryl at South Beach, Miami Reunion in 2009

Virginia, Aunts Clara Arbella, Martha, and Sylvia in Hot Springs, AR

Stone Mountain, Ga. 1st family Reunion picnic 1984

CLOW, AFTER THE GREAT MIGRATION

Estella Shipp & Lizzie Walker

Clow was always a close-knit family community. However, as early as the 1950s, a few Hall descendants began leaving Clow. Lizzie Walker states "Life in the Segregated South was extremely hard: no running water, no indoor toilets, separate schools, working in the field and preparing meals on a daily basis had made life very rough," Some moved and chose towns that bordered Arkansas like Memphis and Hale Center, Texas. Other Halls and Gambles made their way to the highly industrial cities in the North like Chicago, Illinois and Gary, Indiana. Others migrated from small towns like Horatio, Arkansas to Omaha, NE, and New York, while Oakland and Berkeley, California in the West became the choice of others. Clow, of course, has undergone physical changes over the past quarter of a century. Many of us were raised on the three-acre estate of our parents Feazel and Georgia Matlock located at 1185 Hempstead 37 in Ozan, AR.

Home of the Matlock family

The Union Pacific Railroad train would stop very close to our house and would pick up and drop off local residents and at times the deceased bodies of those in Clow and nearby communities who were being returned for burial. The cemetery is located approximately two miles down the railroad track. We have a number of family members buried there including, Aunt Sedelia, Uncle CC and Aunt B, my parents, Bertram,

Bobbie, and others. Also buried there next to uncle CC's gravesite is "Papa Hall"s tombstone. There was an image of his face carved into it. Unfortunately, it is believed that a "right winged" group came through and defaced the headstone. Tall weeds now cover much of the burial grounds.

After the migration, prominent families like the Stewarts, the Browns, the Gambles and the Harris families remained closely connected in Clow. A few years ago if we were to take a stroll through Clow, we would leave my parents' home at 1185 Hempstead, cross the railroad tracks and over the next four blocks on the dirt road we would find three Churches; the Church of God in Christ, a Baptist Church, and Wiley Chapel United Methodist Church. This is the chapel where Rev. CC Hall's funeral was held. There was also a Mason Hall. Our parents also had a store built across the track that had a gas pump. This was the first in Clow to have a gas pump. But the store was more than a place to buy essentials, it became a community center, it had a front porch where people could share the news that was brought in on the Union Pacific Railroad train, and even had a jukebox and dancing in the back room.

Annually, the main social event in Clow was the 4th of July celebration. Stands were set up and people poured in from all neighboring communities. At the end of the road was the Clow Training School. Mother made sure that even if we lived in Memphis or Hale Center Texas, we would return to finish high school here.

THE HALL FAMILY MILITARY HONOREES

Ron Matlock

David Hall Sr,

Lee Ransaw

Terry "Max" Thomas

Freddie Matlock

Xynipher Hall

Charles Brice

Billy Melton

Lonnie Thomas, Sr

William "Bill" Dennis

Millard Haynes

Herbert Randolph Foster

SCHOLASTIC ACHIEVEMENT HONOREES

Judge Bryan Porter

SCHOLASTIC ACHIEVEMENT HONOREES

Dr. Lee Ransaw, Dean

Dr. Vanessa White

The Honorable Shirley Dennis

Dr. Pamela Ayo Yetunde

THE GREAT HALL - GAMBLE FAMILY REUNIONS

Atlanta, GA 1984 the first family reunion

Omaha, NE The third family Reunion 1988

Thelma Gamble

It should be noted that **Thelma Helen (Gamble) Hammonds**, the daughter of Oscar Gamble Jr. and Eva Bertha Gamble, was our first Keynote speaker at the 1984 inaugural family reunion in Atlanta, Georgia. She represented the Gambles while Annie Mary Scoggings was the speaker giving a historical overview of the Halls. Thelma was a graduate of Roosevelt High School in Gary, Indiana and received a B.S. Degree from Philander Smith College in Little Rock, AR. and a master's degree in Elementary Education from the University of Arkansas.

Philadelphia, Pa.

Reunion on South Beach, Miami Florida 2009

Las Vegas, NE 1992

Kansas City Reunion

Las Vegas 2ND Hall- Gamble Reunion

Gary Reunion

ACKNOWLEDGEMENTS

Shirley M. Dennis: I want to thank my cousin Dr. Lee Ransaw for asking me to tell our branch of the Hall family story. It was an exciting opportunity to delve into our history for an extended period of time. The project was supposed to take about 30 days however it took nearly 5 months.

Aunt Martha provided me with important census data and other research done by Gilbert Scoggins, whom I believe knows more than most of us about the Hall, Bryant (my grandmother Elmira Bryant Hall's family), and Gambles' families.

I am grateful for my daughter, Robin for doing much of the ancestral research; Pamela suggesting we look at funeral programs and marriage certificates for some of the information that I needed. Sherry also provided some useful ideas for framing the narrative.

Finally, it is important for me to encourage other branches of the Hall, Bryant and Gamble families, who have not already written their story, to do so. We must tell our stories, even if the information is incomplete. It gives us a starting point. Love to the relatives.

Lizzie Jean Matlock Walker: As a proud family, we grew up loving and appreciating one another. As we celebrate these reunions, let's never forget our past, and keep everyone in our hearts and prayers.

Estella Matlock Shipp: We learned from their examples of love, patience, understanding, perseverance, humility, and kindness. Although many of us are in different places, our love for each other is strong and helps us keep in touch and offer words of encouragement.

Lee A. Ransaw**:* This book is the result of *a divine vision* ***so I must thank our family writers who worked diligently to tell their wonderful stories. I realize that I probably pressed some pretty hard, but once they dug in, they dug deep and now we now have a historical, informative and entertaining document that we can pass on to our descendants.

Hall/Gamble Descendants

Hall/Gamble Descendants

Hall/Gamble Descendants

Made in the
USA
Columbia, SC

81503409R00077